Coffee Recipe

Written by Kim Ji-Hyun

JN412588

Secret recipes for beginners
Let's make at home - Secret recipes from cafe menus

1. All Iced recipes are 14oz (410ml) per serving.

2. All Hot recipes are 10oz (300ml) per serving.

3. Adjust the recipe according to the vessel you are using for the drink.

4. One shot of espresso is 30ml.

5. Use store-bought ones for the syrups and powders not listed in the book.

Contents

Basic menu

Syrup & Powder

Syrup & Sauce

How to Make Espresso Using Espresso Machine

Tip

Pouring out some heated water at the first step is necessary because by doing so, the coffee grounds stuck on the shower screen are removed.

1. Detach the portafilter from the group head and pour out some heated water.
2. Wipe water from the portafilter with a napkin.
3. Grind coffee beans in the grinder and scoop them into the portafilter.
4. With a dry hand, even out the ground coffee.
5. Level out the coffee grounds with a tamper.
6. Dust off the grounds around the portafilter
7. Attach the portafilter onto the group head.
8. Extract 30ml of espresso.
9. Detach the portafilter from the group head.
10. Discard the used coffee grounds in the knock box.
11. Dust off coffee grounds left on the portafilter before re—attaching it back to the group head. Then attach it back.

How to Make Espresso Using Moka Pot

Container

Boiler

Basket

Filter

Upper Gasket

1. Fill the detached boiler with filtered water up to just below the pressure valve.

2. Fill the basket with ground coffee (espresso-grind), and press down with the scoop.

3. Put the basket onto the boiler.

4. Reattach the container with the boiler. (Screw them tight together for no leakage.)

5. Set the fire to low and boil with the lid open.

6. With the sound of water boiling, espresso will start to fill the container.

7. Pour espresso into a preheated cup.

How to Make Espresso Using Cafflano Kompresso

Piston Set

Chamber

Basket

Cup

Scoop

Shower Screen

1. Grind coffee beans finer than espresso grind.
2. Fill the basket with coffee grounds.
3. Level the coffee with the scoop lightly pushing down.
4. Place the shower screen at the bottom of the chamber and screw in the basket.
5. Attach the basket with the chamber to the cup.
6. Pour 50ml of hot water into the chamber.
7. Insert chamber to the piston set and slowly push down to extract espresso.
8. Pour out espresso into a preheated cup.

How to Make Coffee by Hand-drip

Server

Coffee Filter

Dripper

1. Prepare 20g of coffee beans by grinding.
2. Put in the filter to the dripper, put them over a server, and pour hot water over them to warm up.
3. Discard the water in the server. Put the coffee grounds into the filter.
4. Level out the grounds. In a thin stream, pour in hot water drawing circles clockwise, from the center to outward.
5. When the grounds rise, wait for 30 seconds.
6. From the second pouring of hot water, do the same as the first pouring but in a thicker stream.
7. When 200ml of coffee is made after the third pouring, pour the coffee into a preheated cup.

How to Make Cold Brew

Coffee recipes

Coffee Grounds 30g, Filtered Water 300ml, Coffee Filter, A Cup of Ice

1. In a sterilized container, pour in coffee grounds and cold water.
2. Stir and let coffee steep for 12~18 hours in the fridge.
3. Filter out the grounds.

Tip

The size of grounds should be hand-drip grind. Coffee to water ratio is 1:10, or 3:7, in case of wanting heavier taste.

How to Make Steamed Milk and Whipped Cream

Pitcher

Double–froth
Screen Milk
Frother

Electric Frother

1) Electric Frother

– Steamed Milk

1. Put milk in a cup and microwave for 1 minute and 30 seconds.

2. Pour milk in the pitcher and froth it with the electric frother.

– Whipped Cream

1. Pour 100ml of full cream and 10g of caster sugar in a cup and whip it with the electric frother.

2) Double–froth Screen Milk Frother

1. Pour milk in a cup and microwave for 1 minute and 30 seconds.

2. Pour warmed up milk in the frother pitcher. Rapidly pump it with the screen for 20~30 seconds, all the way from the bottom of the pitcher to the surface of milk.

3. Remove the screen and scrap off the froth.

Simple Syrup

Sugar 300ml, Hot Water 300ml

1. The ratio of sugar and hot water is 1 : 1
2. Pour 300ml of sugar and 300ml of hot water in a container and stir.
3. When sugar dissolves, cool down and move to a sterilized container. Store in a fridge.

Tip

You can store it at room temperature, but it can be spoiled. Best stored refrigerated.

Vanilla Syrup

3 vanilla beans, Sugar 400ml, Water 600ml.

1. Cut the vanilla bean in half vertically. Prepare it by scraping it with the back of a knife.

2. Pour water in a pot and boil it with the scraped beans and the pods.

3. When it starts to boil, pour in sugar and keep boiling while stirring continuously.

4. Cool down, pour in a sterilized container. Leave in the fridge to mature for 3 days.

Strawberry Syrup

 ### 14 Frozen Strawberries, Simple Syrup 300ml

1. Put frozen strawberries in a container.
2. Pour in simple syrup and store at room temperature for 4 hours, lid closed.
3. Smash the strawberries with a fork.
4. Move to a sterilized container.

Tip

Use cold syrup that had been stored in a fridge. When you use hot syrup, the strawberries won't break down easily.

Caramel Sauce

(1) Caramel Sauce

Brown Sugar 200ml, Water 50ml, 1tsp Salt, Whipping Cream 200ml

1. Pour brown sugar and salt in a pot
2. Pour in water and boil until the edge turns into the color of caramel.
3. Pour in whipping cream, which has been heated in a double boiler, and stir while boiling for 5 minutes.
4. When everything boils up, turn off the heat and cool down.
5. Put in a sterilized container and store in a fridge.

(2) Easy Caramel Sauce

8 Milk Caramels, Hot Water 20ml

1. Put 8 milk caramel in a microwave-safe container.
2. Pour in 20ml of hot water and microwave for 1 minute.
3. Stir with a spoon. Use in a drink.

Chocolate Sauce

Dark Chocolate 100g, Cocoa Powder 80g, Sugar 180g, Milk 250g

1. Pour milk in a pot and boil.
2. Turn the heat to low. Put in dark chocolate and melt it while stirring.
3. Turn off the heat, put in cocoa powder and sugar. Mix.
4. When all ingredients have dissolved, bring up the heat to boil.
5. Turn off the heat completely, cool off and quickly whisk it.
6. Store in a sterilized container, in a fridge.

Tip

If you use cream instead of milk, the sauce gets richer.

Basic menu

Espresso / Macchiato / Espresso Con Panna

Iced Americano / Cold Brew / Cold Brew Latte

Cold Foam-ccino / Iced Caff Latte / Flat White / Cappuccino

Cold Brew Cube Latte / Shakerato / Iced Cappuccino

Affogato / Coffee Soda / Coffee Lemon Coke

Cream-ccino / Ice Cream Latte

1) Espresso

 ## One Shot of Espresso

1. Preheat the cup with hot water.
2. Extract espresso with a utensil of your choice.
3. Pour out espresso into the preheated cup.

Tip

Try espresso with a spoonful of sugar. Put a teaspoon of sugar in and wait until it sink to the bottom.

You can enjoy layers of espresso: bitter first taste, sweet after-taste.

2) Macchiato

A Shot of Espresso, Steamed Milk 25ml, Milk Froth 15ml

1. .Preheat the cup with hot water.
2. Extract espresso with a utensil of your choice
3. Pour steamed milk in the center slowly and add milk froth on top.

Tip

Macchiato means "to dot" in Italian, in other words, you dot the espresso with milk froth.

Put in a spoonful of sugar, do not stir and enjoy as it is.

You can enjoy softened espresso.

Also, if you are ordering in a coffee shop, you must say espresso macchiato.

Otherwise, you might get caramel macchiato.

3) Espresso Con Panna

One shot of espresso, Whipping cream 30ml, Sugar 3g

1. Whip cream and sugar together.

2. Pour out espresso into a preheated cup.

3. Put whipped cream on espresso.

Tip

Spoon whipped cream with espresso before it melts when you are drinking this.

Enjoy the harmony of cold and smooth cream and warm espresso.

4) Iced Americano

2 shots of espresso, Filtered water 125ml, A cup of ice

1. Pour in a cup of ice into a   cup.

2. Pour in filtered water into the cup.

3. Extract espresso with a utensil of your choice. Pour it in the cup.

Tip

Drink it with a lot of ice.

It will be your best tip to drink americano colder and stronger.

5) Cold Brew

Undiluted Cold Brew, A cup of ice.

1. Pour ice into a cup.
2. Pour in the cold brew coffee.

6) Cold Brew Latte

Cold brew coffee 150ml, Milk 100m, A half cup of ice

1. Pour ice into a cup.
2. Pour in cold brew coffee and fill up with milk.

7) Cold Foam-ccino

▓▓▓ Cold brew coffee 150ml, Whipping cream 100ml, Sugar 10g, A half cup of ice

1. Pour ice into a cup.
2. Pour in the cold brew coffee.
3. Whip cream and sugar together and pour in the coffee slowly.

8) Iced Cafe Latte

▥ **2 shots of espresso, Milk 150ml, A half cup of ice**

1. Pour ice into a cup
2. Pour in milk.
3. Pour in extracted espresso.

9) Flat White

||||| 2 shots of espresso, Steamed milk 120ml

1. Pour espresso into a preheated cup.

2. Pour in steamed milk slowly.

3. Put a thin layer of milk froth on top.

Tip

Flat white is a warm drink that uses a 6oz (180ml) sized cup from which you can enjoy a rich flavor.

10) Cappuccino

One shot of espresso, Steamed milk 150ml, Milk froth, Cinnamon powder 1g

1. Pour espresso into a preheated cup.
2. Pour in steamed milk and put plenty of frothed milk on top.
3. Sprinkle it with cinnamon powder.

11) Cold Brew Cube Latte

8 cubes of frozen cold brew coffee, Milk 180ml

1. Freeze cold brew coffee in an ice mold.
2. Put frozen coffee in a cup.
3. Pour in milk.

12) Shakerato

2 shots of espresso, Filtered water 150ml, A half cup of ice.

1. Put filtered water and ice in a blender and blend.
2. Put espresso into the blender and blend for 3 seconds.
3. Pour in a drinking cup through a filter.

Tip

You can enjoy a sweet version of shakerato with vanilla syrup.

13) Iced Cappuccino

2 shots of espresso, Milk 125ml, Cinnamon powder 1g, Milk froth,
A half cup of ice

1. Pour ice in a cup.
2. Pour in milk.
3. Pour in espresso.
4. Put plenty of frothed milk on the drink.
5. Sprinkle cinnamon powder on top.

14) Affogato

2 shots of espresso, 2 scoops of vanilla ice cream, coffee grounds 1g

1. Chill a cup with some ice.
2. Scoop in 2 scoops of vanilla ice cream.
3. Sprinkle coffee grounds on top.
4. Pour in espresso right before you are serving.

15) Coffee Soda

2 shots of espresso, Sparkling water 150ml, A half cup of ice.

1. Pour ice into a cup.
2. Pour in sparkling water.
3. Pour in espresso.
4. Top off with applemint.

Tip

Use the herd of your preference.

16) Coffee Lemon Coke

2 shots of espresso, Cola 100ml, Lemon, A half cup of ice

1. Squash half a lemon.

2. Pour ice and lemon juice into a cup.

3. Pour in cola.

4. Pour in espresso.

Tip

You can make it sweeter by adding in simple syrup.

17) Cream-ccino

2 shots of espresso, Milk 125ml, Whipping cream 100ml, Sugar 10ml, Cinnamon powder 1g, a half cup of ice.

1. Put ice in the cup
2. Pour in milk and espresso.
3. Whip cream and sugar together. Put it on the drink.
4. Sprinkle cinnamon powder on top.

Tip

whip the cream until stiff, and scoop with an ice cream scoop.

18) Ice Cream Latte

2 shots of espresso, Milk 125ml, 2 scoops of vanilla ice cream, coffee ground, a half cup of ice.

1. Put ice in a cup.
2. Pour in milk and espresso.
3. Add vanilla ice cream on top.
4. Sprinkle coffee grounds.

Syrup & powder

Iced Vanilla Latte / Vanilla Latte / Hazelnut Cappuccino / Maple Latte

Iced Condensed-milk Latte / Coffee Sorbet Ade / Honey Latte

Iced Almond Americano / Iced Almond Latte / Churros-ccino / Orange Cappuccino

Co-co-nut(Coffee Coconut Smoothie) / Green Tea Shot Latte / Earl Grey Shot Latte

Iced Misugaru Shot Latte / Salted Cream Latte / Coffee-mix Coffee

Matcha Viennese Coffee / Strawberry Viennese Coffee / Strawberry Vanilla Latte

Matcha Strawberry Cream Latte

1) Iced Vanilla Latte

Coffee recipes

||||| 2 shots of espresso, Vanilla syrup 30ml, Milk 125ml, A half cup of ice

1. Put ice in a cup.
2. Pour vanilla syrup and milk in.
3. Pour in espresso.

Syrup_powder 69

2) Vanilla Latte

One shot of espresso, Vanilla syrup 20ml, Steamed milk 220ml.

1. Pour vanilla syrup in a preheated cup.
2. Pour steamed milk in.
3. Pour espresso in.

3) Hazelnut Cappuccino

One shot of espresso, Hazelnut syrup 20ml, Steamed milk 150ml, Milk froth

1. Pour hazelnut syrup in a preheated cup.
2. Pour in espresso.
3. Pour in steamed milk.
4. Top off with plenty of frothed milk.

4) Maple Latte

One shot of espresso, Maple syrup 20ml, Steamed milk 220ml

1. Pour maple syrup in a preheated cup.

2. Pour in espresso.

3. Pour in steamed milk.

5) Iced Condensed Milk Latte

2 shots of espresso, Condensed milk 30ml, Milk 150ml,
A half cup of ice

1. Pour ice in a cup.

2. Pour in condensed milk

3. Pour in milk and espresso.

6) Coffee Sorbet Ade

3 shots of espresso, Maple syrup 150ml, Filtered water 400ml, Sparkling water 150ml, A cup of ice

1. Mix maple syrup, filtered water, 3 shots of espresso.
2. Freeze it for 5 hours.
3. Pour ice in a cup.
4. Pour in sparkling water.
5. Scrape the coffee sorbet with a fork, scoop, and put on the drink.

Syrup_powder **79**

7) Honey Latte

One shot of espresso, Honey 30ml, Steamed milk 220ml

1. Pour honey in a cup.

2. Pour steamed milk in.

3. Pour espresso in.

8) Iced Almond Americano

Coffee recipes

2 shots of espresso, Almond syrup 20ml, Simple syrup 10ml, Filtered water 150ml, Plenty of ice.

1. Fill the cup with ice.
2. Pour almond syrup and simple syrup in.
3. Pour filtered water in.
4. Pour espresso in.

9) Iced Almond Latte

▥ 2 shots of espresso, Almond syrup 20ml, Simple syrup 10ml, Milk 150ml, Plenty of ice

1. Pour ice in a cup.
2. Pour almond syrup and simple syrup in.
3. Pour milk in.
4. Pour espresso in.

10) Churros-ccino

One shot of espresso, Sugar 30g, Cinnamon powder 1g, Steamed milk 150ml, Milk froth

1. Put cinnamon powder and sugar in a preheated cup.
2. Pour in steamed milk and stir.
3. Pour in espresso.
4. Add plenty of frothed milk.
5. Sprinkle it with cinnamon powder and sugar.

11) Orange Cappuccino

One shot of espresso, A half of orange, Simple syrup 20ml, Steamed milk 150ml, Milk froth

1. Squeeze a half of an orange into a preheated cup.
2. Pour in simple syrup.
3. Pour in espresso.
4. Pour in steamed milk and put plenty of frothed milk on top.
5 Put a slice of orange on the drink..

Syrup_powder 89

12) Co-co-nut(Coffee Coconut Smoothie)

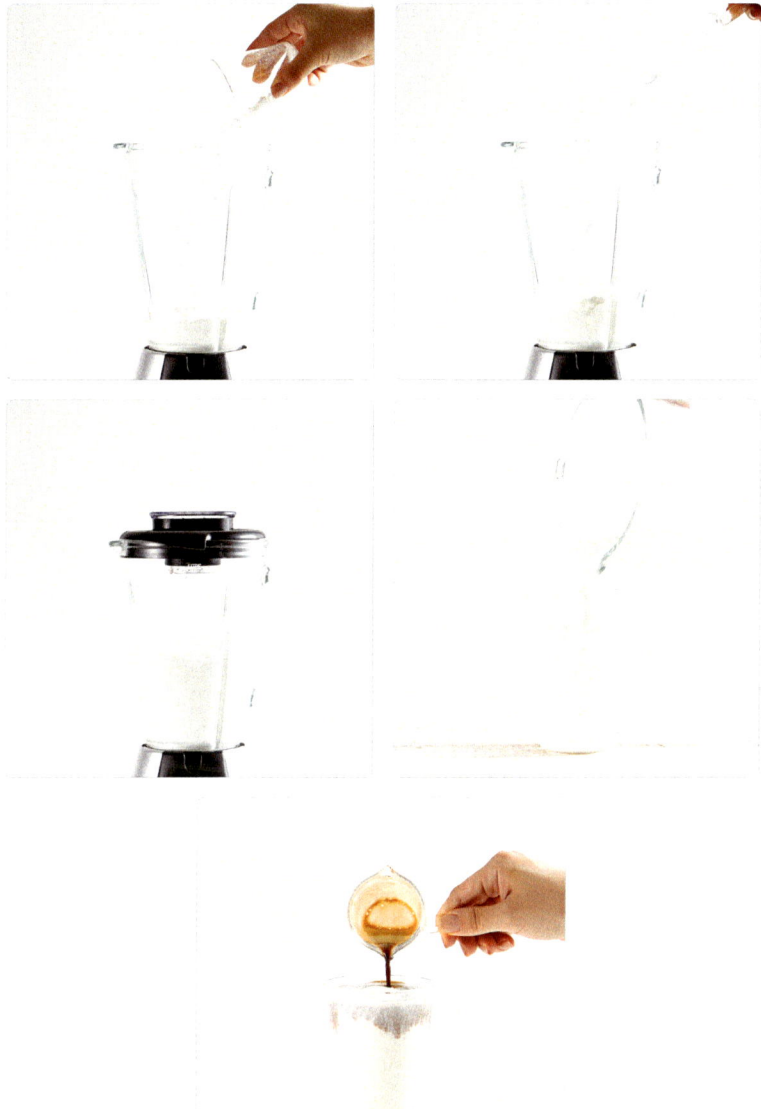

2 shots of espresso, Cocoa powder 50g, Milk 120g, A cup of ice.

1. Put milk, cocoa powder, and ice into a blender and blend.
2. Pour the blended mix into a cup.
3. Pour in espresso.

13) Green Tea Shot Latte

One shot of espresso, Green tea powder 25g, Steamed milk 220ml

1. Put in green tea powder in a preheated cup.

2. Pour in steamed milk and stir.

3. Pour in espresso.

4. Sprinkle green tea powder on top.

14) Earl Grey Shot Latte

Coffee recipes

Earl Grey tea 3g, One shot of espresso, Simple syrup 10ml, Steamed milk 220ml

1. Steep Earl Grey tea in hot water for 3 minutes.
2. Pour the tea and sugar in a preheated cup.
3. Pour in steamed milk.
4. Pour in espresso.

Syrup_powder

15) Iced Misugaru Shot Latte

One shot of espresso, Misugaru 30g, Simple syrup 30ml, Water 50ml, Milk 100ml, A half cup of ice

1. Put misugaru, water, and milk in a cup. Whisk.
2. Pour simple syrup and put ice in the cup.
3. Pour espresso in.

16) Salted Cream Latte

Coffee recipes

 2 shots of espresso, Whipping cream 100ml, Sugar 10g, Salt 1g, Milk
 150ml, A half cup of ice

1. Pour ice in a cup.

2. Pour milk and espresso in.

3. Whip the cream, sugar, salt together. Top off the drink with it.

Syrup_powder

17) Coffee-mix Coffee

▥ 2 shots of espresso, Vanilla syrup 15ml, Filtered water 100ml, Milk 50ml, A half cup of ice.

1. Pour ice in a cup.
2. Pour in vanilla syrup.
3. Pour in filtered water and milk.
4. Pour in espresso.

Syrup_powder **101**

18) Matcha Viennese Coffee

2 shots of espresso, Matcha powder 5g, Simple syrup 10ml, Whipping cream 50ml, Water 150ml, A half cup of ice

1. Pour ice in a cup.
2. Pour in water and espresso.
3. Mix the cream with matcha powder and simple syrup. Whip them together. Pour in the cup.
4. Sprinkle matcha powder on top.

19) Strawberry Viennese Coffee

▥ 2 shots of espresso, Strawberry syrup 15ml, Whipping cream 50ml, Water 150ml, A half cup of ice.

1. Pour ice in a cup.

2. Pour water and espresso in.

3. Whip the cream with strawberry syrup. Pour in.

20) Strawberry Vanilla Latte

▒ 2 shots of espresso, Strawberry syrup 20ml, Vanilla syrup 10ml, Milk 150ml, A half cup of ice

1. Put ice in a cup.

2. Pour in strawberry syrup, vanilla syrup, and milk.

3. Pour in espresso.

21) Matcha Strawberry Cream Latte

2 shots of espresso, Strawberry 25ml, Matcha powder 5g, Simple syrup 10ml, Whipping cream 50ml, Milk 150ml, A half cup of ice.

1. Put ice in a cup.
2. Dissolve matcha powder and simple syrup in hot water and pour in the cup.
3. Pour in espresso.
4. Whip strawberry syrup with cream and pour in the cup.
5. Whip strawberry syrup with cream and pour over.

Syrup & sauce

Iced Caramel Macchiato / Iced Cafe Mocha / Iced Mint Mocha / Caramel Popcorn Smoothie

Chocolate-loaded Latte / Cinnamon Chocolate Latte / Iced Strawberry Mocha

Iced Blue Mocha / Salted Caramel Latte / Almond Mocha-ccino / Macaron Cream Latte

1) Iced Caramel Macchiato

 *Coffee recipes*

2 shots of espresso, Caramel sauce 15ml, Vanilla syrup 20ml, Milk 150ml, Milk froth, A half cup of ice

1. Pour caramel sauce and vanilla syrup into a cup.
2. Pour in milk and stir.
3. Put ice in and put milk froth on top of it.
4. Slowly pour in espresso. Drizzle with caramel sauce.

2) Iced Cafe Mocha

2 shots of espresso, Chocolate sauce 20ml, Vanilla syrup 10ml, Milk 150ml, A half cup of ice

1. Pour chocolate sauce and vanilla syrup in a cup.

2. Pour in espresso and stir.

3. Put ice in the cup.

4. Pour in milk.

5. Whip some whipping cream and top the drink with it.

6. Drizzle with chocolate sauce.

3) Iced Mint Mocha

2 shots of espresso, Chocolate sauce 15ml, Mint syrup 20ml, Milk 150ml, A half cup of ice

1. Pour chocolate sauce in a cup.
2. Put in ice and pour milk in.
3. Pour mint syrup in.
4. Pour espresso in.

Syrup_sauce 117

4) Caramel Popcorn Smoothie

Coffee recipes

▓ 2 shots of espresso, Caramel sauce 30ml, Vanilla syrup
  10ml, Milk 100ml, Whipping cream 100ml, sugar 10g, 10
  kernels of caramel popcorn

1. Pour milk in a blender.
2. Add caramel sauce and vanilla syrup to it.
3. Pour in espresso.
4. Put in some ice and blend.
5. Put the blended drink in a cup. Whip the cream and sugar
   together and top the drink with it.
6. Top off with caramel popcorns and drizzle with caramel sauce.

5) Chocolate-loaded Latte

One shot of espresso, Chocolate sauce 20ml, Steamed milk 200ml, Dark chocolate.

1. Pour chocolate sauce and steamed milk in a cup and stir.

2. Pour espresso in.

3. Top it with milk froth.

4. Chop up dark chocolate and load the drink with it.

6) Cinnamon Chocolate Latte

One shot of espresso, Chocolate sauce 15ml, Cinnamon powder 1g, Steamed milk 220ml.

1. Put chocolate sauce and cinnamon powder in a preheated cup.
2. Pour in steamed milk and stir.
3. Pour espresso in.
4. Put a thin layer of milk froth on top of it and drizzle with chocolate sauce.
5. Sprinkle cinnamon powder on top of it.

7) Iced Strawberry Mocha

▒▒ 2 shots of espresso, Strawberry syrup 20ml, Chocolate sauce 15ml, Milk 150ml, A half cup of ice.

1. Pour chocolate syrup and strawberry syrup in a cup.
2. Put ice in and pour in milk.
3. Pour in espresso.

8) Iced Blue Mocha

2 shots of espresso, Blue curacao syrup 10ml, Chocolate sauce 20ml,
Milk 150ml, A half cup of ice.

1. Pour chocolate sauce in a cup.
2. Put ice in.
3. Pour in milk.
4. Pour in blue curacao syrup.
5. Pour espresso in.

9) Salted Caramel Latte

▥ One shot of espresso, Caramel sauce 20ml, Salt 1g,
   Steamed milk 220ml.

1. Put caramel sauce and salt in a preheated cup.

2. Pour in steamed milk and stir.

3. Top with milk froth and pour in espresso.

4. Drizzle with caramel sauce and sprinkle with a little salt.

10) Almond Mocha-ccino

One shot of espresso, Chocolate syrup 15ml, Almond syrup 10ml, Chocolate powder 1g, Steamed milk 150ml, Milk froth.

1. Pour chocolate syrup and almond syrup in a cup.
2. Pour in steamed milk and stir.
3. Top it with plenty of milk froth.
4. Pour in espresso.
5. Sprinkle chocolate powder on top.

11) Macaron Cream Latte

▥ 2 shots of espresso, 3 macarons, Simple syrup 10g, Blue curacao syrup 10g,
Whipping cream 100ml, milk 150ml, A half cup of ice.

1. Crush the macarons and put in a cup.
2. Pour in simple syrup and ice.
3. Pour in milk.
4. Pour in espresso.
5. Whip the cream with blue curacao syrup and top the drink with it.
6. Crush a macaron and top off with it.

Coffee Recipes

First Printing : 7th July 2024.
First Published : 15th July 2024.

Written by Kim Ji—Hyun
Published by Kim Tae—Heon
Publisher Star Five

Address : 53, Daesan—ro, Ilsanseo—gu, Goyang—si, Gyeonggi—do,
Republic of Korea

Copyright : 11 th March, 2021. 2021—000062

Telephone : 031—911—3416
Fax : 031—911—3417